W9-CAB-190

ALL NEW
Crafts
for
Mother's Day
and Father's Day

KATHY ROSS
Illustrated by Sharon Lane Holm

M Millbrook Press   Minneapolis

To my own mother
and father with
lots of love!
—K.R.

Millbrook Press, Inc.
A division of Lerner Publishing Group
241 First Avenue North
Minneapolis, MN 55401 U.S.A.

Website address: www.lernerbooks.com

Library of Congress Cataloging-in-Publication Data

Ross, Kathy (Katharine Reynolds), 1948–
   All new crafts for Mother's Day and Father's Day / by Kathy Ross ; illustrated by
Sharon Lane Holm.
      p.   cm. — (All new holiday crafts for kids)
   ISBN-13: 978–0–8225–6367–9 (lib. bdg. : alk. paper)
   ISBN-10: 0–8225–6367–3 (lib. bdg. : alk. paper)
   1. Holiday decorations. 2. Handicraft—Juvenile literature. 3. Mother's Day—
Juvenile literature. 4. Father's Day—Juvenile literature. I. Holm, Sharon Lane. II.
Title. III. Series: Ross, Kathy (Katharine Reynolds), 1948– All-new holiday crafts for
kids.
   TT900.H6R66 2007
   745.594'1628—dc22   2006001313

Manufactured in the United States of America
1 2 3 4 5 6 – JR – 12 11 10 09 08 07

Contents

This gift is perfect for the pet-loving parent!

Pet Tape Dispenser

Here is what you need:

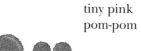

clear plastic cellophane
tape dispenser with tape

two wiggle eyes

felt scrap

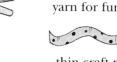
glue

white craft glue

tiny pink
pom-pom

1½-inch (3.8-cm) pom-pom and
two ½-inch (1.25-cm) pom-poms

scissors

yarn for fur

thin craft ribbon

thread

Here is what you do:

1 Decide if you want to make a cat or a dog for your parent. If there is a pet at your house, then you might want to choose yarn and pom-pom colors similar to that pet.

2 Pop the tape off the dispenser and remove the paper liner.

3 Cover the print side of the paper liner with glue and yarn snips for the fur.

4

4 When the glue has dried, place the liner back in the tape dispenser so that the yarn fur is visible through the plastic.

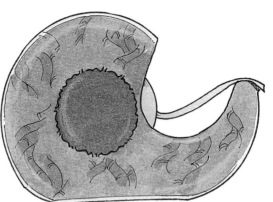

5 Snap the roll of tape back into the dispenser.

6 Glue the large pom-pom into the hole in the dispenser for the head of the pet.

7 Glue the two small pom-poms at the bottom of the tape dispenser, below the head, for the paws.

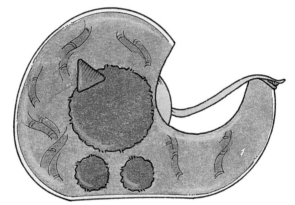

8 Cut small triangles of felt for cat ears. Dog ears are usually larger. See sample dog on the next page. Glue the ears to the top of the head.

9 Glue the wiggle eyes to the front of the head.

(continued on next page)

10 Cut two or three 2-inch (5-cm) threads for the cat whiskers. You'll want dog whiskers to be shorter. Glue them to the front of the head below the eyes.

2"

11 Glue the pink pom-pom over the center of the threads for a nose.

12 Trim the ends of the whiskers to make them even.

13 Make a small bow from the thin craft ribbon. Glue the bow at the neck of the pet.

You might want to add a little jingle bell to the ribbon at the neck.

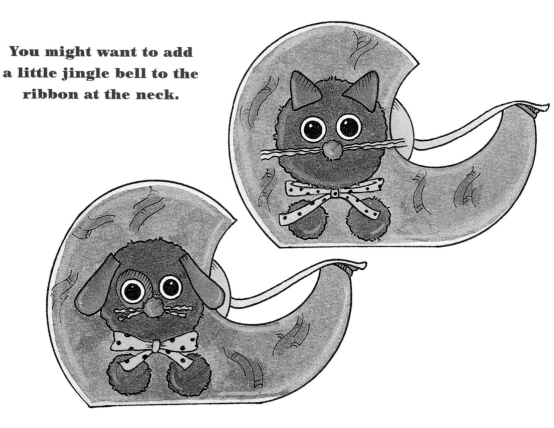

Give Mom or Dad the gift of kisses and hugs!
Xs mean kisses, and Os mean hugs!

Xs and Os Magnets

Here is what you need:

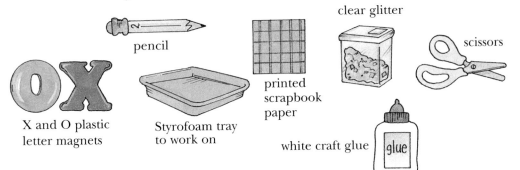

pencil

clear glitter

scissors

printed scrapbook paper

X and O plastic letter magnets

Styrofoam tray to work on

white craft glue

glue

Here is what you do:

1 Place each letter face down on the back of the printed paper, and trace around it with a pencil.

2 Cut each letter shape out.

3 Glue each paper shape, print side up, to the front of the matching plastic letter.

4 Place the letters on the Styrofoam tray. Cover the front of each letter with glue and sprinkle with the clear glitter. Let the glue dry.

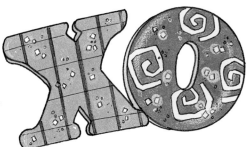

Instead of tracing, you can color the top of a letter with a washable marker. Then print the shape on the back of the printed paper. Wipe the marker clean before gluing the paper on it.

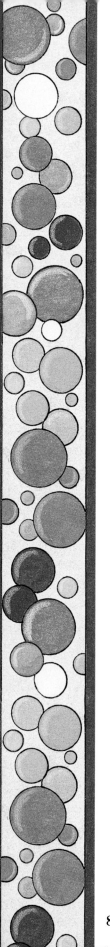

Make an ordinary jar extraordinary with this project!

Jazzy Jar Cuff

Here is what you need:

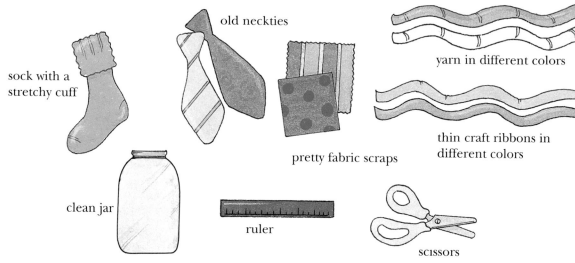

sock with a stretchy cuff

old neckties

yarn in different colors

pretty fabric scraps

thin craft ribbons in different colors

clean jar

ruler

scissors

Here is what you do:

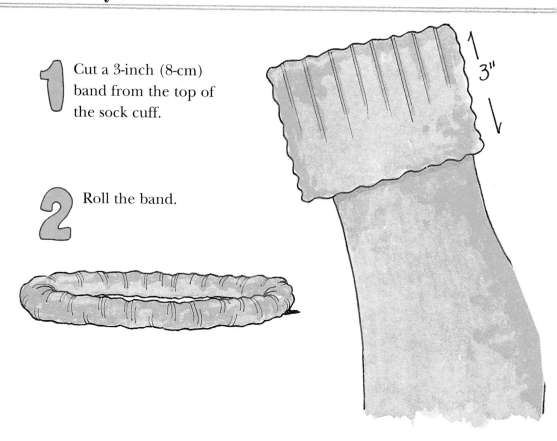

1 Cut a 3-inch (8-cm) band from the top of the sock cuff.

3"

2 Roll the band.

8

3 Cut eight to ten 1- by 5-inch (2.5- by 13-cm) strips of fabric. You can use printed fabric for your mom or fabric cut from old neckties for your dad.

4 Cut several 5-inch (13-cm) lengths of ribbon and/or yarn.

5 Tie the fabric and the ribbon and/or yarn pieces around the rolled cuff. Add more strips of fabric and ribbon if needed.

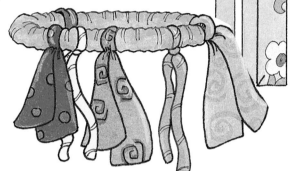

6 Slip the cuff over the rim of the jar to decorate it.

Decorated jars make attractive and useful storage containers in many household areas, from the shop to the computer desk!

Try your hand at making this gift idea!

Little Hands Notepad

Here is what you need

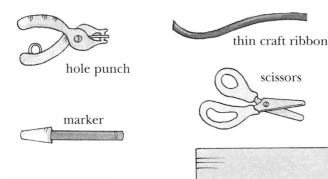

hole punch

thin craft ribbon

scissors

variety of printed
paper in light colors

marker

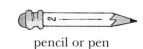
pencil or pen

ruler

poster board

Here is what you do:

 Use the pencil or pen to trace around one
of your hands on the poster board.

 Cut the hand shape out.

Use the shape as a pattern and trace
around it on the printed paper. Cut
about twenty hand shapes from the
paper. You might want to cut a
stack of three or four paper
hands at one time.

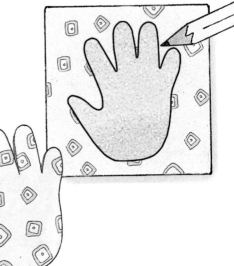
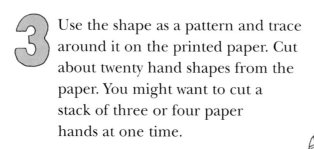

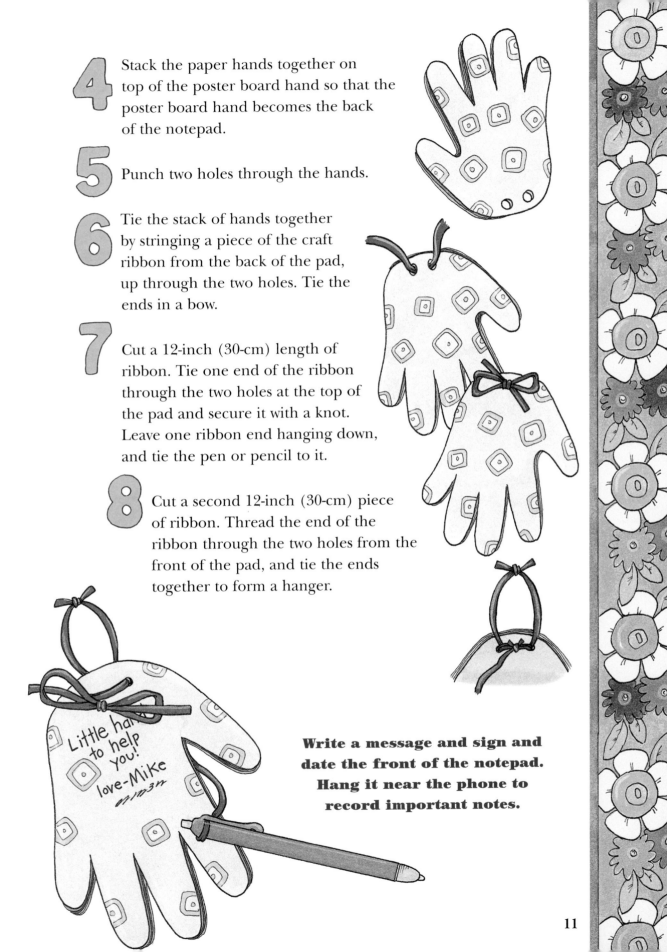

4 Stack the paper hands together on top of the poster board hand so that the poster board hand becomes the back of the notepad.

5 Punch two holes through the hands.

6 Tie the stack of hands together by stringing a piece of the craft ribbon from the back of the pad, up through the two holes. Tie the ends in a bow.

7 Cut a 12-inch (30-cm) length of ribbon. Tie one end of the ribbon through the two holes at the top of the pad and secure it with a knot. Leave one ribbon end hanging down, and tie the pen or pencil to it.

8 Cut a second 12-inch (30-cm) piece of ribbon. Thread the end of the ribbon through the two holes from the front of the pad, and tie the ends together to form a hanger.

Write a message and sign and date the front of the notepad. Hang it near the phone to record important notes.

Little hand to help you! love-Mike

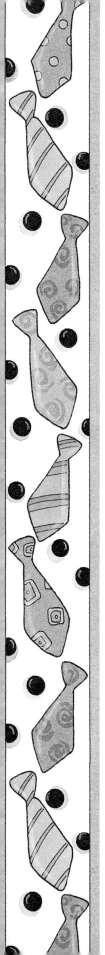

Make a gift for Mom or Dad using a photo of you!
Photo Ornament

Here is what you need:

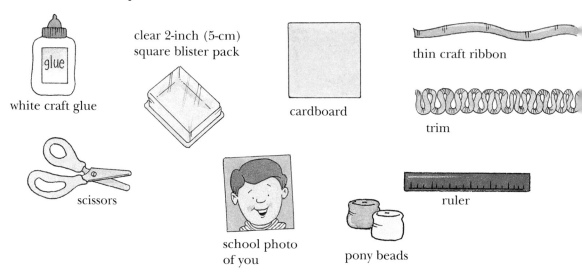

white craft glue

clear 2-inch (5-cm) square blister pack

cardboard

thin craft ribbon

trim

scissors

school photo of you

pony beads

ruler

Here is what you do:

1. Place the blister plastic on the cardboard backing. Cut the cardboard along the edge of the plastic so that the cardboard will become the backing for the plastic square. Do not be concerned if the paper sticks a little to the flat edges of the blister pack as this will be concealed in a later step.

2. Trim the photo to fit exactly on the cardboard backing.

3. Cut a 20-inch (51-cm) length of the craft ribbon.

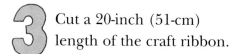

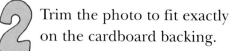

12

4 Fold the ribbon in half. Glue it down in the center of the cardboard so that the top half of the ribbon forms a loop hanger and the two ends hang down from the bottom of the cardboard.

5 Glue the photo to the backing over the ribbon.

6 Glue the plastic blister pack over the photo to cover and protect it.

7 Slide two or three pony beads over the ribbon at the top and the bottom of the photo. If they do not stay in place, secure them with a dab of glue.

8 Glue trim around the flat edge of the blister pack to cover it.

This photo ornament looks nice hanging on a bulletin board or window hook.

Make this quick and easy photo display for a desk or table.

Flower Photo Holder

Here is what you need:

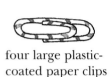

four large plastic-coated paper clips

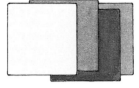

construction paper in four colors

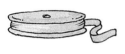

green vinyl tape

scissors

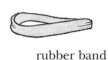

rubber band

mesh bag of craft stones

ruler

four artificial flowers with 8- to 10- inch (20- to 25-cm) stems

Here is what you do:

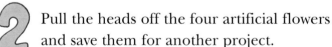

1 Tighten the bag of craft stones by wrapping the rubber band around one end of the bag to make it smaller.

2 Pull the heads off the four artificial flowers and save them for another project.

3 Attach a paper clip to the top of each stem using the vinyl tape.

14

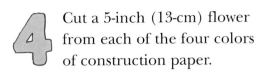

4 Cut a 5-inch (13-cm) flower from each of the four colors of construction paper.

5 Slip a flower in each paper clip to serve as a backing for each photo.

glue photo here

You can add the photos to the flowers yourself, or let your mom or dad pick their own favorites to display.

This comfy pillow can change decorations with the seasons!

Changing Theme Pillow

Here is what you need:

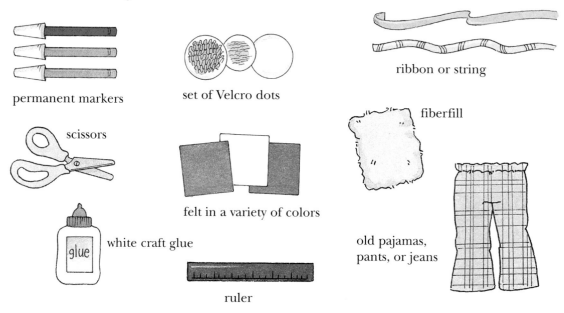

permanent markers

scissors

white craft glue

set of Velcro dots

felt in a variety of colors

ruler

ribbon or string

fiberfill

old pajamas,
pants, or jeans

Here is what you do:

1 Make the pillow from old pajamas, pants, or jeans, selecting a fabric you think your parent would like.

2 Cut a 16-inch (41-cm) or longer tube from the leg for the pillow.

3 Close off the tube by tying a ribbon or string around one end of it.

4 Stuff the tube with fiberfill. Then tie the other end closed with ribbon or string.

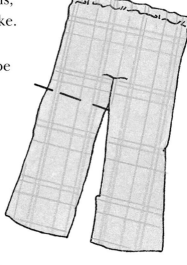

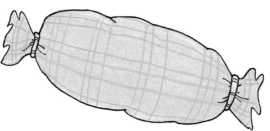

5 Trim the excess fabric at the end of each pillow so that each end is even.

6 Decide what theme the decorations will be. You might make decorations for different sports or different seasons or holidays.

7 Cut 4- to 5-inch (10- to 13-cm) shapes from the felt. For sports you might cut out a football, a race car, and a baseball. Make shapes to represent the sports your parent likes to play or watch. For the seasons, you might cut out a leaf, snowflake, flower, and sun. Or you could cut simple shapes for the holidays your family celebrates. To add details, use a permanent marker to draw directly on the shape or cut additional felt pieces and glue them on the front.

(continued on next page)

8 Press the fuzzy side of a Velcro dot on the center of the pillow. Press the hook side of a Velcro dot on the back of each shape you make.

The decorations on the pillow can be changed by carefully separating the Velcro dots and attaching a different shape.

Mom would love a set of these pretty food covers to use at a summer picnic.

Picnic Food Cover

Here is what you need:

twelve large, odd clip-on or pierced earrings

three fabric napkins in colors that look nice together

Here is what you do:

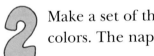

1 Attach an earring to each corner of the napkin to use as a weight. The earrings can be either clip-on or pierced, but they should be heavy enough to weigh down the corners of the napkin.

2 Make a set of three food covers in complementing colors. The napkins can be different sizes.

These food covers will be a welcome addition at any picnic! The earrings are easily removed so the covers can be washed.

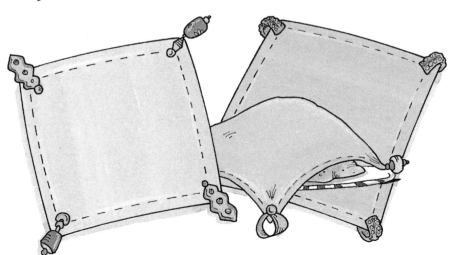

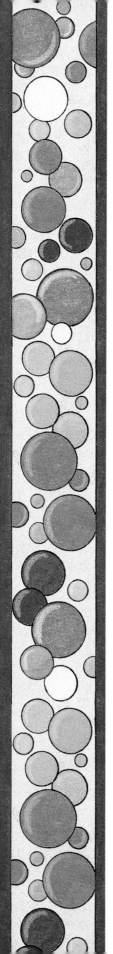

Your dad will be marking his place in style with this gift idea!

Necktie Bookmark

Here is what you need:

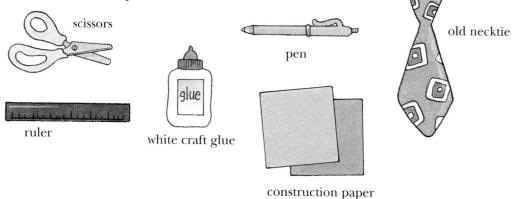

scissors

ruler

white craft glue

pen

construction paper

old necktie

Here is what you do:

1 Cut a 10-inch (25-cm) piece from the thin end of the old necktie.

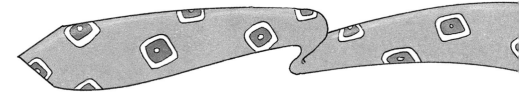

2 Knot the cut end of the tie to look like a tied necktie.

3 Secure the knot with glue.

4 On the construction paper, trace with the pen to trace around the portion of the tie below the knot .

5 Cut the shape out. It should cover the back side of the necktie without the edges showing in front, so you may need to trim the edges of the paper shape slightly.

6 Write a Father's Day message on the paper tie shape.

I love you, Daddy!
Happy Father's Day!
love, chris

7 Glue the shape to the back of the tie.

I love you, Daddy!
Happy Father's Day!
love, chris

North Wind

This bookmark is so clever, your mom might want one too!

These handy packets of lotion are perfect
for stashing in a purse or travel kit.

Travel Lotion Packets

Here is what you need:

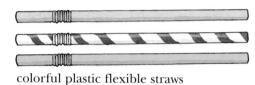

colorful plastic flexible straws

clear packing tape

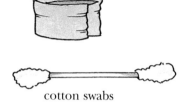

cotton swabs

lotion in a
pump bottle

plastic
sandwich bag

thin craft ribbon

scissors

Here is what you do:

1 Fold over the flexible end of the straw to close the end off.

2 Hold the open end of the straw under the lotion
bottle spout, pushing the end up into the spout as
much as possible to seal any gaps.

3 Pump the lotion firmly into the straw. You may have
some leak out the sides, depending on the shape of
the spout.

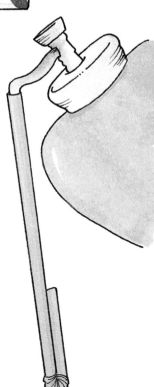

4 Cut the end off a cotton swab.

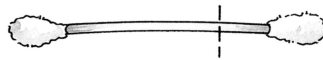

5 When the straw is almost full of lotion, seal off the end by inserting the end cut from the cotton swab.

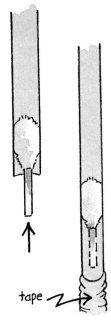

6 Wrap a strip of clear packing tape over the end of the straw. Wrap more tape around the end of the straw to secure it.

tape

7 Tie the folded end of the flexible straw shut with a piece of craft ribbon tied in a bow or knot. To use the lotion, the ribbon will need to be untied and the top of the straw unfolded. The lotion can then be squeezed from the straw.

8 Make three or more packets of lotion.

9 Place the lotion packets in the plastic bag. Tie the bag shut with another piece of craft ribbon tied in a pretty bow.

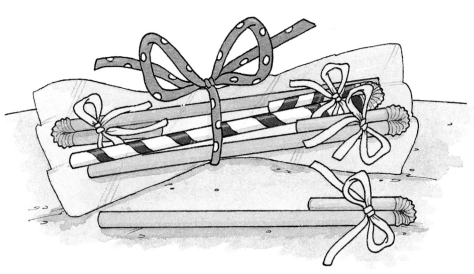

If you are making a set of travel lotion packets for your dad, you might want to use twine instead of craft ribbon, to give the packets a more masculine look.

Feathery Dresser Dish

Here is what you need:

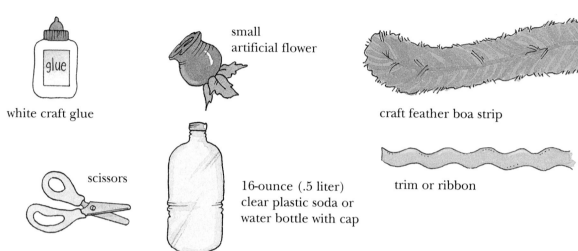

white craft glue

small artificial flower

craft feather boa strip

scissors

16-ounce (.5 liter) clear plastic soda or water bottle with cap

trim or ribbon

Here is what you do:

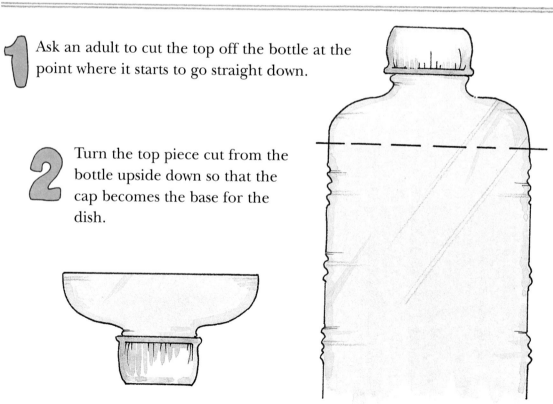

1. Ask an adult to cut the top off the bottle at the point where it starts to go straight down.

2. Turn the top piece cut from the bottle upside down so that the cap becomes the base for the dish.

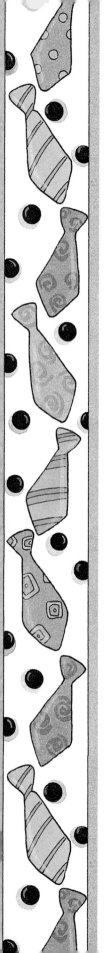

3 Cover the outside of the cap by gluing on a piece of the trim or ribbon.

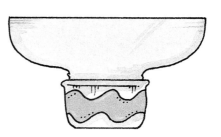

4 Cover the rest of the dish with glue, and wrap the feather boa strip around and around to cover it. Trim off the excess feather boa strip from the end.

5 Glue a small flower to the side of the feather-covered dish.

How fancy!

Make this dish for Dad's dresser or desk.

Photo Dresser Dish

Here is what you need:

 scissors

 felt

 two identical clear plastic soda or water bottles

 school photo of you

colored vinyl tape

Here is what you do:

1 Ask an adult to cut the bottom half off each bottle to use for the dish.

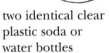
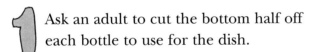

2 Cut a strip of felt to line the inside of one of the bottle bottoms.

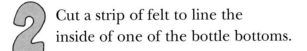

3 Slip the photo of you into the bottle bottom between the felt and the bottle so that it can be seen through the side of the dish.

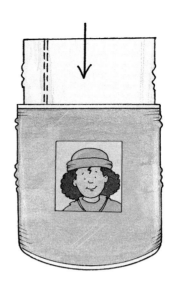

4 Cut a slit down the side of the other bottle, and then cut the bottom out of it. Trim the top and bottom slightly so that it just fits inside the dish to form a plastic liner inside the felt liner.

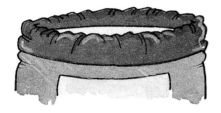

5 Cover the top edge of the dish by folding a strip of the vinyl tape over the entire top edge.

This container is perfect for holding pens, pencils, loose change, and other small odds and ends that end up on a dresser or desk.

These markers help avoid beverage mix-ups with a crowd.

Bottle and Cup Markers

Here is what you need:

poster board

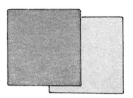

pen

craft foam in different colors
for each marker you make

scissors

suction cups with
small hooks on end

Here is what you do:

1 Use the pen to draw a simple
3-inch (8-cm) flower shape
on the poster board.

2 Cut the shape out
to use as a pattern.

3 Use the pen to trace the flower
pattern on each color of craft
foam you are using.

 Cut each flower out.

 Remove the hook from each suction cup.

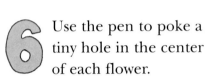 Use the pen to poke a tiny hole in the center of each flower.

7 Slip each flower over the bump on the front of a suction cup where the hook was removed.

The suction cups will allow the flowers to stick to a glass, plastic cup, or bottle, making it easy for guests to recognize their own beverage.

These flowers really belong in the shower!

Scrubbie Bouquet

Here is what you need:

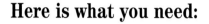

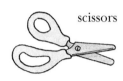
scissors

colored tissue paper

large jar

ribbon

one or more mesh shower scrubbies

wire stems and leaves from artificial flowers

Here is what you do:

1   If the flower stems you are using still have flower heads on them, pull the flowers off to save for another project.

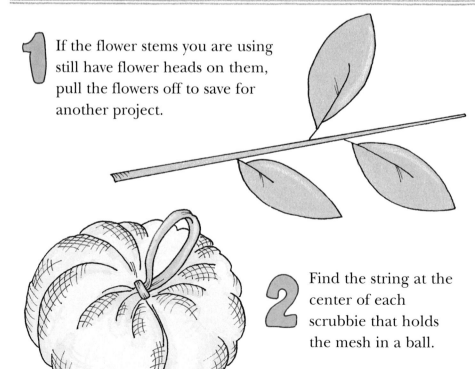

2   Find the string at the center of each scrubbie that holds the mesh in a ball.

3 Slip the end of a flower stem through the center string of a scrubbie to make a flower.

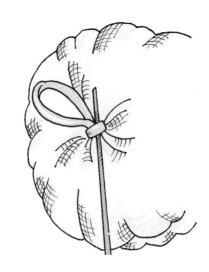

4 Tie the ribbon in a pretty bow around the neck of the jar.

5 Cut three large squares of the tissue paper to bring up around the stem or stems of the flowers.

6 Place the flowers in the jar.

The flowers are easily pulled off the ends of the stems to use in the shower.

Your mom will love wearing this pretty pin!

Vintage-Look Pin

Here is what you need:

white craft glue

scissors

green felt scrap

safety pin

pink
blue
yellow

ruler

large-size seed beads
for flower centers

pink, blue, and yellow
skeins of embroidery floss

Here is what you do:

1 To make the flowers, tie each full skein of embroidery floss into a loose knot at the center.

2 Tuck both ends of the skein into the knot and secure with dabs of glue.

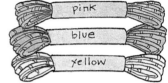

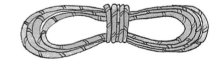

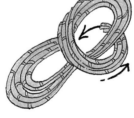

3 Glue several seed beads in the center of each flower to finish.

4 Cut two 3-inch (8-cm) leaves for the flowers from the green felt.

5 Glue the two ends of the leaves together.

6 Glue the three flowers to the center where the two leaves meet.

7 Slip a safety pin through the center of the back of the leaves while the glue is still wet.

You might want to choose other colors for the flowers you make for your mom.

Make your dad feel really special with this gift idea!

#1 Dad Doorknob Hanger

Here is what you need:

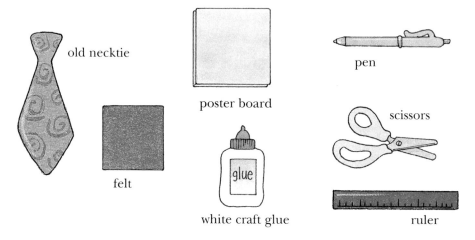

old necktie

poster board

pen

felt

white craft glue

scissors

ruler

Here is what you do:

1 Cut a 12-inch long (30-cm) piece from the wide end of the necktie.

2 Use the pen to trace around the necktie end on the poster board.

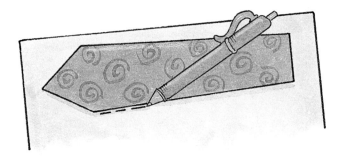

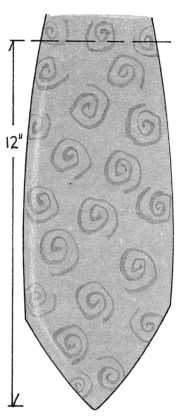

12"

3 Cut the traced shape out.

4 Trim the edges of the poster board shape slightly so that it will just fit inside the tie.

 5 Rub a very thin layer of glue on both sides of the poster board tie shape.

poster board

6 Slip the poster board in between the front and the back of the tie.

7 Cut down from the flat top of the tie about an inch. Then cut a 1½-inch (3.8-cm) circle to allow the tie to hang from behind a doorknob.

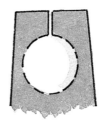

8 Use the pen to write *#1 Dad* on the felt.

9 Cut the message out.

10 Glue the message to the front of the necktie.

You might want to glue a different message on your necktie doorknob hanger.

This pretty air freshener is perfect to hang in the car.

Umbrellas Air Freshener

Here is what you need:

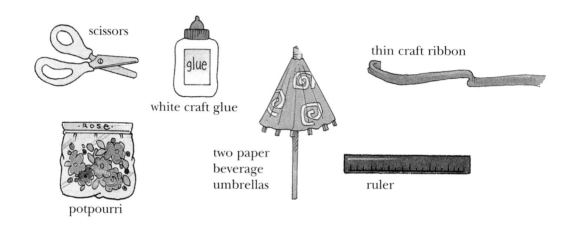

scissors

white craft glue

potpourri

two paper beverage umbrellas

thin craft ribbon

ruler

Here is what you do:

1 Open the two umbrellas as far as you can and cut off the wooden handles.

2 Turn one of the umbrellas upside down and fill it with potpourri.

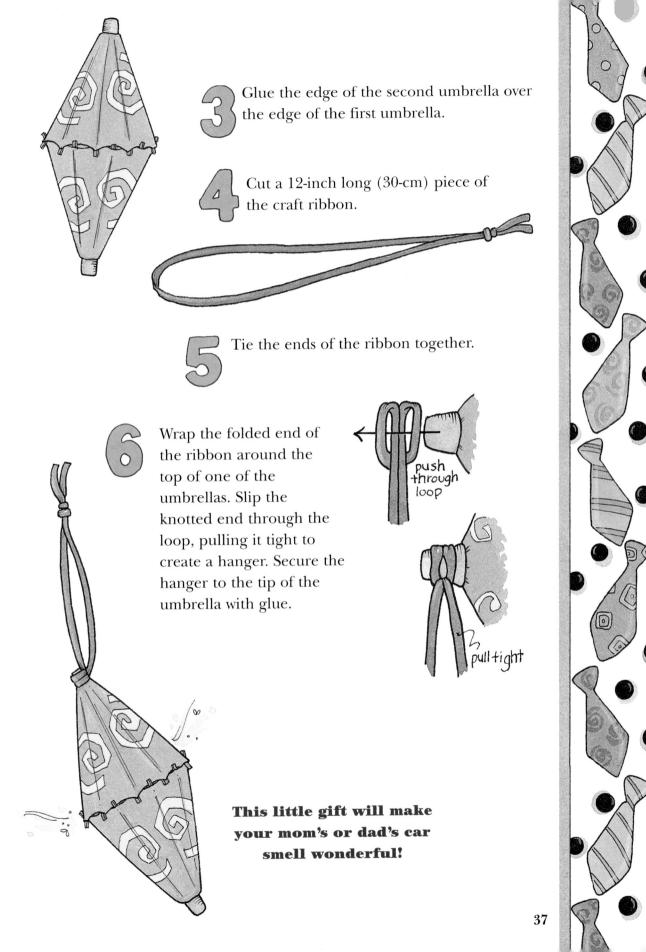

3 Glue the edge of the second umbrella over the edge of the first umbrella.

4 Cut a 12-inch long (30-cm) piece of the craft ribbon.

5 Tie the ends of the ribbon together.

6 Wrap the folded end of the ribbon around the top of one of the umbrellas. Slip the knotted end through the loop, pulling it tight to create a hanger. Secure the hanger to the tip of the umbrella with glue.

push through loop

pull tight

This little gift will make your mom's or dad's car smell wonderful!

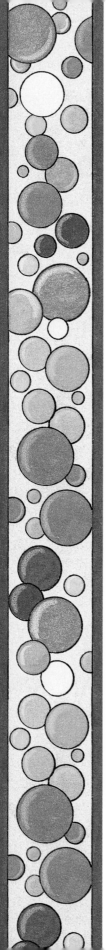

Make this clever card for your dad!

Handsome Dad Father's Day Card

Here is what you need:

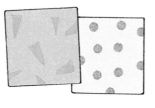

printed paper in two complementary patterns

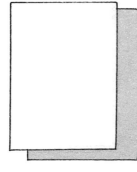

white and green 9- by 12-inch (23- by 30-cm) construction paper

white craft glue

scissors

markers

ruler

Here is what you do:

1. Fold the green construction paper in half to make a 6- by 9-inch (15- by 23-cm) card.

2. Fold the white construction paper in half the same way. Trim about ½ inch (1 cm) off the edges of the white construction paper so that it will fit inside the green card.

3. Glue the white paper inside the green card.

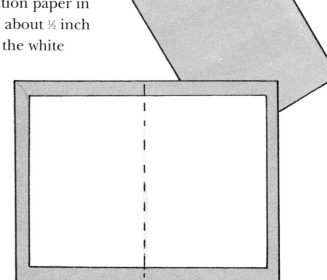

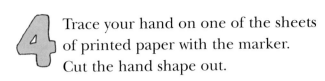

4 Trace your hand on one of the sheets of printed paper with the marker. Cut the hand shape out.

5 Cut a 5- by 7-inch (13- by 18-cm) rectangle from the other sheet of printed paper.

6 Glue the printed paper to the center of the front of the card. Glue the hand shape to the center of the printed paper rectangle.

7 Write the date at the top of the front of the card. Write "My hand . . ." at the bottom of the front of the card.

8 Open the card and write ". . . some dad!" on the inside left, and draw a picture of your dad above it.

9 Sign your name below your message on the right.

Wrapping paper, pads of scrapbook paper, wallpaper, and colorful catalogs are all good sources of printed paper for this project.

**This Mother's Day card comes with a pin for
your mom to remove and wear!**

Card with Pin for Mom

Here is what you need:

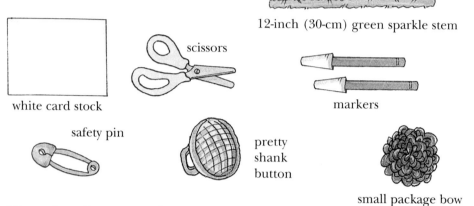

white card stock

scissors

12-inch (30-cm) green sparkle stem

markers

safety pin

pretty
shank
button

small package bow

Here is what you do:

1 Slide the shank button to the center of the
green sparkle stem.

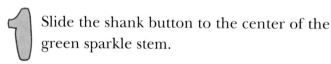

2 Place the button in the center of the bow.
Twist the ends of the sparkle stem together
behind the bow to secure the button.

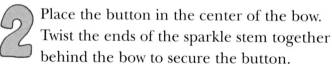

3 Shape the two ends of the sparkle stem
into a leaf on each side of the flower.

4 Slide the back of the safety pin through the sparkle stem at the back of the flower.

5 Fold the card stock and trim it to make a 5- by 6-inch (13- by 15-cm) card.

6 Pin the flower to the upper left corner of the card, and use the markers to draw a stem.

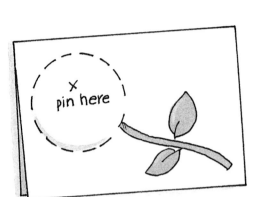

×
pin here

7 Write a Mother's Day greeting on the front of the card. And be sure to write your own special message for your mom inside the card.

Happy Mother's Day!

Your mom will be surprised to find that her card is also a gift to wear!

This spring wreath easily changes decorations for different occasions.

A Wreath for All Seasons

Here is what you need:

 scissors

 plastic snack cup

clear plastic domed deli container that snaps over flat plate

craft ribbon

 white craft glue

green Easter grass

decorations of choice, such as photos, artificial flowers, candy, small ornaments, seashells

hole punch

 ruler

Here is what you do:

1. Cut a hole in the center of the plastic plate that is slightly smaller than the opening of the plastic snack cup.

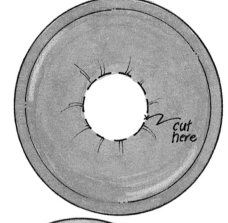
cut here

2. Glue the rim of the snack dish over the hole in the center to create the wreath.

3. Arrange the Easter grass around the wreath. Use enough so that the dome is filled when snapped back on the plate.

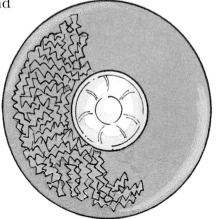

4 Arrange decorations of your choice on the Easter grass wreath.

5 Cut an 18-inch (46-cm) piece of the ribbon.

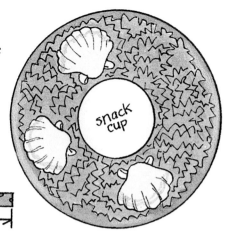

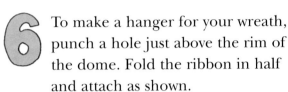
|← —— 18" —— →|

6 To make a hanger for your wreath, punch a hole just above the rim of the dome. Fold the ribbon in half and attach as shown.

7 Snap the dome lid on over the grass, decorations, and hanger to secure them.

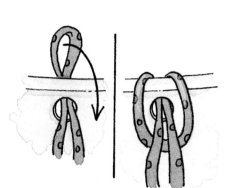

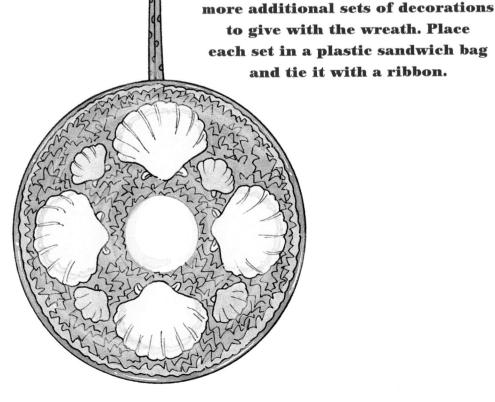

You might want to collect one or more additional sets of decorations to give with the wreath. Place each set in a plastic sandwich bag and tie it with a ribbon.

Make a set of magnets for your mom or dad!

Eraser Magnets

Here is what you need:

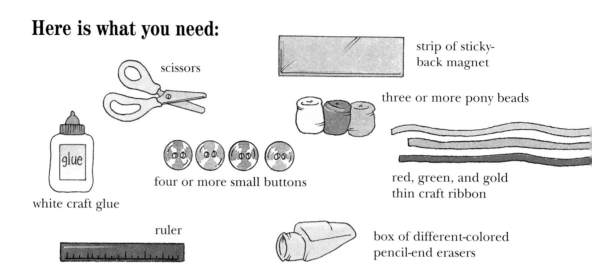

scissors

strip of sticky-back magnet

three or more pony beads

four or more small buttons

red, green, and gold thin craft ribbon

white craft glue

glue

ruler

box of different-colored pencil-end erasers

Here is what you do to make the vase magnet:

1 To make a vase of flowers, cut five 1½- to 2-inch (4- to 5-cm) pieces of the green craft ribbon, and tuck into the opening of an eraser.

├── 1½″ ──┤

├──── 2″ ────┤

2 Slip a bead over three of the ribbons, and secure them with a dot of glue.

3 Press a piece of sticky-back magnet on the back of the eraser vase.

Here is what you do to make the car magnet:

1 Press the end of one eraser into a second eraser to make the car.

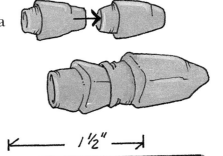

2 Cut three or four pieces of 1½-inch-long (4-cm) red and gold ribbon.

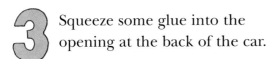

3 Squeeze some glue into the opening at the back of the car.

4 Tuck the ends of the ribbon pieces into the back of the car to look like flame coming out the back.

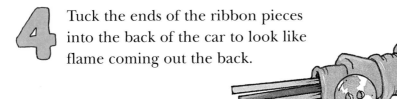

5 Glue two buttons on each side of the car for the wheels.

6 Press a piece of the sticky-back magnet to the bottom of the car.

baseball
3 pm.
Thurs.

milk
cookies

Make a set of three car or vase magnets in different colors.

45

Page markers are a handy thing for your
mom or dad to keep by a favorite reading chair.

Page Markers

Here is what you need:

white craft glue

square
sticky-note
pad

sequins

small pictures or stickers

scissors

ribbons and trims

Here is what you do:

 Peel about six pages off the sticky-note pad.

 Starting at the bottom of the sticky notes,
cut the stack into three equal strips.

 Stick the three strips together to form a
new, narrow pad of sticky notes.

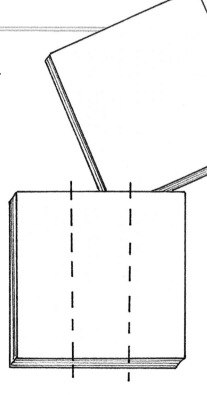

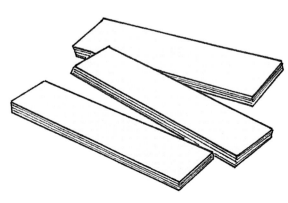

4 Decorate the bottom of each strip by gluing on a tiny picture, sticker, sequin, or strip of ribbon or trim.

5 Use a tiny dot of glue so you do not stick the pages together. If a page is gluey, place a small piece of plastic wrap between the glue and the next page until the glue has dried.

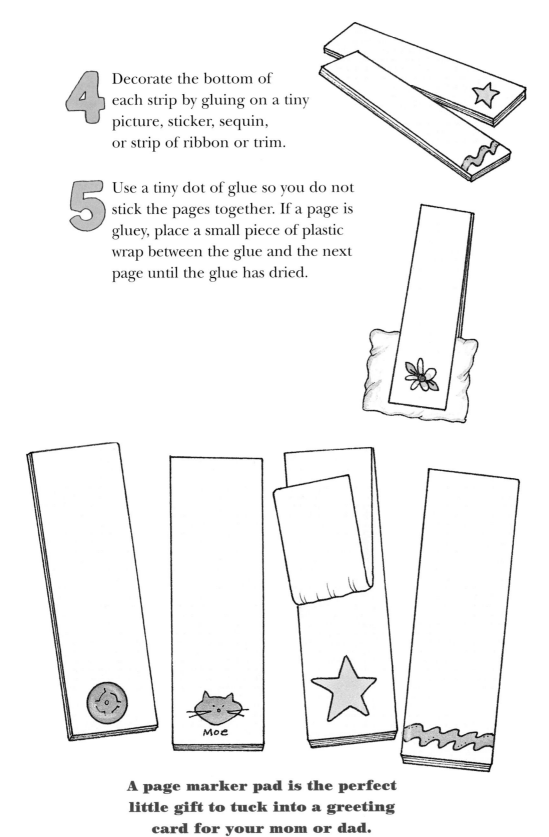

MOE

A page marker pad is the perfect little gift to tuck into a greeting card for your mom or dad.

About the Author and Artist

Thirty years as a teacher and director of nursery school programs have given Kathy Ross extensive experience in guiding young children through craft projects. Among the more than forty craft books she has written are *All-Girl Crafts, The Scrapbooker's Idea Book, Things to Make for Your Doll, Girlfriend's Get-together Craft Book,* and *Crafts for Kids Who Are Learning About* series. To find out more about Kathy, visit her website: www.Kathyross.com.

Sharon Lane Holm, a resident of Fairfield, Connecticut, won awards for her work in advertising design before shifting her concentration to children's books. Her recent books include *Happy New Year, Everywhere!* and *Merry Christmas, Everywhere!* by Arlene Erlbach. You can see more of her work at www.sharonholm.com.

Together, Kathy Ross and Sharon Lane Holm have created *The Best Christmas Crafts Ever!* and *The Big Book of Christian Crafts,* as well as earlier books in this series: *All New Crafts for Easter, All New Crafts for Thanksgiving, All New Crafts for Kwanzaa,* and *All New Crafts for Halloween.*

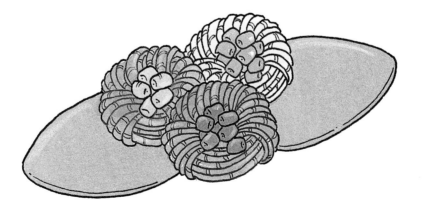